THE BOOK OF ADIRONDACK FIRSTS

By David Cross and Joan Potter

Illustrated by Alison Muñoz

Pinto  Press

Pinto 🐾 Press
Elizabethtown, New York 12932

ISBN 0-9632476-0-3

Library of Congress Catalog Card Number:
92-93333

9 8 7 6 5 4 3 2

For Royal Potter and John Sabol

ADIRONDACK FIRSTS

TABLE
OF
CONTENTS

PREFACE

As amateur historians, we were struck while doing the research for this book by the difficulties and temptations that professional historians must face every day. If history is, as has been written, "a distillation of rumor," then how does one determine the truth about the past?

The early days of the Adirondacks are shrouded by time and colored by the personalities of those who have chronicled regional events. Newspaper accounts were often designed to attract customers, and reporters sometimes embellished or distorted the facts to satisfy the appetites of their readers.

Historians, too, we came to suspect, have particular agendas. Whether to support their own points of view or to repudiate professional rivals, they often draw the wrong conclusions from vague and conflicting material and then interpret the facts to consolidate their findings. Descendants of historical figures sometimes are more motivated to preserve the character of their forebears than to portray them accurately, with their flaws as well as their virtues.

Since our focus was on finding the people, places and events that have entered history because they were the <u>first</u>, we often had to consider conflicting claims. There may be readers who disagree with our choices and historians who dispute our findings, but our goal was to provide an intriguing look at Adirondack history and the people who created it. We hope that this unique perspective on the past will entertain our readers as well as inform them.

We have many people to thank for helping us find and collect our "firsts," including the countless authors of books and magazine and newspaper articles, both past and current, and the local librarians and historians who provided us with time and material. We are especially grateful for the generous assistance of Reid Larson, the director of the Essex County Historical Society; Jerold Pepper, the librarian at the Adirondack Museum in Blue Mountain Lake; Dorothy Irving, archive librarian at the Keene Valley Library; Joseph Swinyer, the special collections librarian at the Feinberg Library of the State University College at Plattsburgh; and Mary MacKenzie, the historian for the Town of North Elba and the Village of Lake Placid. Our special thanks go to John Bradley for his technical expertise.

WHO

WHO WAS IN CHARGE OF THE FIRST COMPLETE SURVEY OF THE ADIRONDACKS?

In 1865, Verplanck Colvin, an outspoken advocate for legislative protection of the Adirondacks, started surveying the region at his own expense. Seven years later he was officially appointed superintendent of the state land survey, and was granted funds to undertake a complete topographical survey of the Adirondack Mountains. Until the state ended the survey eighteen years later, Colvin issued detailed yearly reports. His vivid accounts attracted much public attention and greatly influenced the passage of the Forest Preserve Act of 1885.

15

WHO STARTED THE FIRST ADIRONDACK NEWSPAPER FOR LUMBERJACKS?

Frank Reed was one of six Adirondack "sky pilots" -- ministers of the gospel who traveled by foot, snowshoe, railroad or plane to bring religion, books and supplies into lumber camps.   In 1939, following the suggestion of a lumberjack at Harvey's camp in Nobleboro, Reed created a newspaper called Lumber Camp News. He issued the paper on an experimental basis in January, February and March, attracting 300 paid subscribers, before beginning regular publication in May.

WHO FIRST USED ELECTRICITY IN INDUSTRY?

Allen Penfield, owner of the Irondale iron works in what is now Crown Point, bought a large electromagnet in the late 1820's from Professor Joseph Henry in Albany and used it to make electricity for his iron works. This was the first time in history that electricity was used for industrial purposes.

WHO FIRST COINED THE TERM "FOREST RANGER"?

In 1897, William Fox, the State Superintendent of Forests, called for a change in what he considered an ineffective "firewarden" system used to protect the wilderness from fires. Two years later, after an epidemic of severe forest fires, Fox proposed the establishment of a force of "forest rangers" that would patrol the Adirondack and Catskill wilderness, stamping out any small fires left behind by campers and protecting fish and game from poachers. But the state legislature was unresponsive, and it wasn't until 1912 -- long after the devastating Adirondack forest fires of 1903 and 1908 -- that a law was passed setting up a permanent force of forest rangers.

WHO DROVE THE FIRST AUTOMOBILE INTO THE ADIRONDACKS?

While traveling on their honeymoon in July of 1902, a Buffalo couple, Mr. and Mrs. Herbert J. Sackett, drove the first automobile into the Adirondack region and spent some time at Lower Saranac Lake and Paul Smiths. It is said that the auto left terror and awe in its path.

WHO FIRST CLIMBED AN ADIRONDACK MOUNTAIN ON SKIS?

In 1911, two General Electric officials, Nobel Prize winner Irving Langmuir and John Apperson, an Adirondack environmentalist, ascended Mt. Marcy wearing skis. The feat was repeated one year later on Whiteface Mountain by Fridtjof Nansen, a Norwegian scientist, author, and explorer.

WHO WAS THE FIRST POSTMASTER IN KEENE?

In 1823, David Graves was appointed the first postmaster of the first post office in Keene Center, located at the Graves Hotel. Carried by horseback from Westport, the mail was delivered twice a week.

WHO FLEW THE FIRST AIRMAIL FROM THE ADIRONDACKS?

Born in Willsboro Point in 1893, Dr. Alphonzo Goff practiced medicine in Keene Valley for 59 years, often flying to remote areas in his own plane. On May 19, 1938, Dr. Goff flew the first airmail out of the Adirondacks, carrying a bag of 800 letters from Keene Valley to Albany. A small airfield in Keene Valley, Marcy Field, was dedicated in 1974 to the beloved doctor, who was known for never refusing to treat patients regardless of their ability to pay and for never sending out a bill.

WHO WAS THE FIRST WHITE MAN IN THE ADIRONDACKS TRIED FOR THE MURDER OF AN INDIAN?

Nat Foster, a famous 19th-century hunter and trapper, was arrested and tried for the murder of the Indian Drid, whom he shot to death from a point of land just below First Lake as Drid paddled past in his bark canoe. Foster was indicted on February 3, 1834, in the Herkimer County Court but, despite all the evidence against him, his two-day trial ended in an acquittal. Drid -- who was also known as Peter Waters -- was buried at Old Forge, his grave marked by a simple cross inscribed "Pete".

WHO WAS THE FIRST ADIRONDACK GUIDE?

While there may have been others before him, John Cheney is the first guide to be written about in the early chronicles of the region. In 1830, he arrived in the Adirondacks with a dog, a gun, and a pack basket and earned his living in the mountains as a guide until the age of 73. Cheney, described as "one of the mildest, most unassuming, pleasant men to be met with anywhere," is noted for having led the party of Ebenezer Emmons on the first recorded ascent of Mt. Marcy in 1837.

WHO MADE THE FIRST ATTEMPT TO TURN THE ADIRONDACKS INTO A NATIONAL PARK?

In a June 1885 article in the American Nationalist, William Hosea Ballou wrote: "Will anyone say that the Government of the United States ought not to be charged with the care of the portions of these aged relics which a great State has given over to weeds and bandits?" No one took up his suggestion until July 30, 1967, when Laurance S. Rockefeller, who was chairman of the State Council of Parks, proposed the creation of an Adirondack Mountains National Park. If his plan had been accepted, the park would have included 1,720,000 acres, making it the third largest national park in the country. Although Rockefeller's brother Nelson was then governor of New York State, the proposal never got off the ground.

WHO MADE THE FIRST RECORDED ASCENT OF MT. MARCY?

In 1837, Professor Ebenezer Emmons of Williams College, while surveying the Adirondack region, headed a party that made the first recorded ascent of Mt. Marcy, the tallest of the High Peaks. The group was led by two well-known guides, John Cheney of Tahawus and Harvey Holt of Keene Valley. Emmons named the mountain after the governor of New York, William Learned Marcy, who had proposed the survey.

WHO WAS THE FIRST WOMAN TO BELONG TO THE ADIRONDACK FORTY-SIXERS?

Grace L. Hudowalski first climbed Mt. Marcy on a rainy, foggy day in 1922. When she finally reached the summit and caught a glimpse of Lake Tear-of-the-Clouds, the 15-year-old Hudowalski was hooked. She went on to become the first woman to climb Mt. Allen and the first female member of the Adirondack Forty-Sixers, an organization of people who have climbed all 46 peaks over 4,000 feet high.

WHO WAS THE FIRST SETTLER IN SARANAC LAKE?

Born in Keene, New Hampshire, in 1787, Jacob Moody was injured in a sawmill accident while still a young man and was forced to find a new career. He resettled in Saranac Lake in 1819, cleared 16 acres of land, and built a log cabin where Mrs. Moody gave birth to the first white child in the region, naming him Cortez. The Moody children became famous guides and one son, Martin, who guided such notables as Ned Buntline, President Chester Arthur and President Grover Cleveland, also opened several hotels.

WHO INVENTED THE FIRST SNOW TIRE?

Having had trouble getting to his cabin at Big Moose, Earl W. Covey, builder, woodsman, guide, innkeeper and inventor, applied crepe rubber to the surface of the tires on his Ford truck. The Firestone Tire and Rubber Company was impressed enough to manufacture Covey's tires on a limited basis in 1929, but because of the short life of crepe rubber, these first snow tires never caught on.

WHO BUILT THE FIRST STONE CASTLE IN THE ADIRONDACKS?

In 1893, on a 9,000-acre estate between Tupper Lake and Long Lake, a New York lawyer and financier, Edward Hubbell Litchfield, built a castle of native stone in the style of a French chateau. The turreted castle had an art gallery and a great hall containing a collection of 193 animal heads. Litchfield constructed an eight-foot wire fence around his property and attempted to raise big game animals such as moose, elk and wild boar. His effort failed when some of the creatures died in captivity and others were killed by poachers or escaped after storms blew the fence down.

WHO WAS THE FIRST DOCTOR IN THE ADIRONDACKS?

Unable to become a Jesuit priest, Rene Goupil instead studied medicine in France and came to this country to become a doctor. He traveled into the Adirondacks with Father Isaac Jogues and was captured by the Mohawks. Legend says he was murdered with a tomahawk in 1642 after making the sign of the cross on the head of an Indian boy.

WHO MADE THE FIRST RECORDED ASCENT OF WHITEFACE?

In 1814, a surveyor named John Richards became the first person on record to reach the top of Whiteface Mountain. This 4,865-foot peak was given its name because of a prominent white slide area near its summit. Later in the century, climbers often scaled Whiteface not on foot, but on horseback.

WHO CREATED THE FIRST BUCKBOARD?

Tired of being bounced about while riding the backroads of the Adirondacks administering to his flock, the Reverend Cyrus Comstock borrowed an idea from the logging wagons he frequently passed. By placing the seat of his buggy on a long flexible plank between the axles of the carriage, he created a smoother ride. Comstock's idea spread like wildfire throughout the entire country.

WHO WERE THE FIRST COUPLE TO BE MARRIED ON THE TOP OF CASCADE MOUNTAIN?

On May 26, 1976, William A. Kozel and Kathleen Ann Lynch were joined together in holy matrimony by the Reverend Philip L. Giles on the top of Cascade's 4,098-foot peak. The wedding party celebrated by consuming a two-tiered cake and, instead of throwing rice at the bride and groom, showered them with birdseed.

WHO CREATED THE FIRST OIL PAINTING OF THE ADIRONDACKS?

While accompanying the geologist Ebenezer Emmons on some of his excursions through the Adirondacks, Charles Cromwell Ingham, a founder of the National Academy of Design, made several sketches, one of which became the basis for a painting titled "The Great Adirondack Pass." Created in 1837, the work became part of the permanent collection of the Adirondack Museum at Blue Mountain Lake.

WHO BUILT THE FIRST ADIRONDACK "SUMMER CAMP"?

A New York City millionaire, Theophilus Anthony, born in 1735, is credited with being the first to build a "summer camp" on his property near Long Lake in 1768. This luxurious structure was the first in a series of millionaire mountain retreats, a tradition that was refined by William West Durant. All that remains of Anthony's camp are traces of the foundation, but three small lakes west of Long Lake still bear his name.

WHO WAS FIRST TO PUBLISH A STUDY OF BIRDS IN THE ADIRONDACKS?

When he was only 12 years old, Teddy Roosevelt spent the summer of 1871 at Paul Smith's Hotel on St. Regis Lake. The lad visited Ausable Falls and took extensive notes on the wildlife, which he published six years later in a pamphlet called "The Summer Birds of the Adirondacks in Franklin County, N.Y." Many years later, in September, 1901, after he had become Vice-President, Roosevelt was descending from Mt. Marcy when he learned that President McKinley, who had been shot a week earlier by an anarchist in Buffalo, was dying. Roosevelt rushed through the night by buckboard to the nearest railway station in North Creek, but before he could board a train for Buffalo, he received word that McKinley had died.

WHO WAS THE FIRST PERSON TO SWIM THE ENTIRE LENGTH OF LAKE GEORGE?

On her third try, Diane Struble (covered with five pounds of grease to keep her warm) swam the entire length of the 32-mile lake. After 35 1/2 hours in the water, Struble came ashore at Beach Road on August 22, 1958, and was greeted by 10,000 cheering fans. Her next feat was crossing Lake Champlain from Burlington to Plattsburgh. The triumphant Ms. Struble then traveled to New York City where she swam around Manhattan Island.

WHO FIRST ADVOCATED THE PROTECTION OF THE ADIRONDACKS?

In 1857, Samuel H. Hammond, an Albany journalist, in a publication entitled "Wild Northern Scenes," stated: "Had I my way, I would mark out a circle of a hundred miles in diameter, and throw around it the protecting aegis of the Constitution, I would make it a forest forever."

WHO WERE THE FIRST TO CLIMB ALL THE HIGH PEAKS?

Two brothers, Robert and George Marshall, with their guide, Herbert Clark, finished climbing all 46 Adirondack peaks over 4,000 feet high on June 10, 1925. Subsequently, an organization called the Adirondack Forty-Sixers was formed by others who had accomplished this feat. The two brothers awarded Haystack Mountain the highest rating for best views, with Marcy, the tallest peak, coming in at number eight.

WHO WAS
THE FIRST EUROPEAN TO
TRAVEL UP LAKE CHAMPLAIN?

In 1609, Samuel de Champlain, accompanying an Algonquin war party from Canada, sailed into the lake now bearing his name. Setting foot on Adirondack soil near Ticonderoga, he fired at a group of Iroquois Indians, killing two, and thus created Indian hostilities that would last for 175 years.

WHO WERE THE FIRST ADIRONDACK LAND SPECULATORS?

In 1771, two Manhattan shipwrights, Joseph Totten and Stephen Crossfield, paid 1,135 pounds for what they estimated to be 800,000 acres of Adirondack land in the area that later became Essex, Hamilton, Herkimer and Warren counties. In their purchase from the indigenous Indians, Totten and Crossfield were merely acting as agents for the real buyers, land speculators Edward and Ebenezer Jessup. Later surveys found that this parcel of land was much bigger than presumed -- it actually contained more than 1.1 million acres.

WHO WAS THE FIRST WELL-KNOWN HERMIT IN THE ADIRONDACKS?

The mysterious Moses Follensby, the first "professional" hermit, lived west of Saranac Lake by the pond that now bears his name. Born in England in 1749, Follensby had a reputation for being an honest man as well as a shiftless vagabond and poor hunter. Vivid rumors followed Follensby's sudden disappearance in 1823. It was reported that his gun and dog were left at home and the remains of a meal for two were still on his table. One historian wrote that a wooden chest was found in Follensby's cabin, containing a diamond-studded sword in a gold scabbard, gold toilet articles, and a decorated, scarlet British uniform coat. Others claimed that the recluse was a French marquis and a veteran of Napoleonic wars.

WHO WAS THE FIRST GIRL TELEPHONE OPERATOR IN THE ADIRONDACKS?

When William A. Dana retired from the switchboard at Colonel Baker's Hotel in Saranac Lake, he was replaced by fourteen-year-old Estella Manning. For this work, the young girl was paid one dollar a week plus room and board.

WHO WAS FIRST TO RECORD A VISIT TO AUSABLE CHASM ?

In October 1765, William Gilliland discovered and described in his journals the now famous natural gorge. "It is," he wrote, "a most admirable sight, appearing on each side like a regular built wall, somewhat ruinated. One would think this prodigious cleft was occasioned by an earthquake."

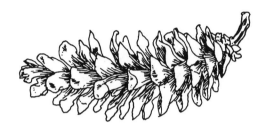

WHO WAS THE FIRST PRESIDENT OF THE ESSEX COUNTY HISTORICAL SOCIETY?

Formed in 1954, the fledgling society elected Harry MacDougal to serve as president. His first act was to find the deed for the old high school, which mandated the building be used only for educational purposes. The board of education then set the price of the building at one dollar, and the society purchased it for its headquarters and the home of the Adirondack Center Museum. MacDougal also served as Essex County Clerk for 33 years and was the Elizabethtown Supervisor for seven years.

WHO IS CONSIDERED THE FIRST "ADIRONDACK INNKEEPER"?

In 1832, George Rockwell, the first in a line of colorful Adirondack hoteliers, opened a hotel in Lake Luzerne that was frequented by tourists from Saratoga Springs. He advertised his hostelry, which was constructed of logs, as a "large three-story building divided up into pleasant high-walled rooms in suits."

WHO WAS THE FIRST PROTESTANT MINISTER IN THE ADIRONDACKS?

In 1765, George Henry came from New York City to Willsboro. He was the first person officially placed in charge of a parish in the North Country.

WHO WAS THE FIRST SETTLER IN JAY?

In 1795, Nathaniel Mallory and 34 other pioneers settled at the falls on the Ausable River in Jay. Granted 640 acres for a total of 501 pounds, Mallory built a gristmill and served as justice of the peace. The town was called Mallory's Bush until 1800 when its name was changed to Jay, after the then-governor of New York, John Jay.

WHO BUILT THE FIRST ADIRONDACK GUIDEBOAT?

Credit for creating this unique craft is usually given to Mitchell Sabattis, an Abenaki Indian guide who worked in the Long Lake region in the 1800's. In 1850, Sabattis's pupil, Caleb Chase, set up a shop in Newcomb and built Adirondack guideboats for 40 years. About 16 feet long and weighing 75 pounds, this boat had to be both sturdy enough to transport equipment and men across water and light enough to be carried across land. Five thousand tacks and three thousand screws went into the construction of each boat, making it a truly rugged vessel.

WHO WAS THE FIRST STEAMBOAT PILOT ON LAKE CHAMPLAIN?

At the helm of the "Vermont" when she was launched in 1809, Hiram Ferris served as the first pilot on the lake. Born in Vermont in 1792, Ferris never had an accident. He discovered a rocky reef, which now bears his name, opposite the present Port Kent, and served as pilot until 1859.

WHO WAS THE FIRST SETTLER IN KEESEVILLE?

In 1802, Robert Hoyle settled in what is now Keeseville, building the first bridge and the first sawmill and opening a general store called "The Long Chute."

WHO WERE THE FIRST SETTLERS OF LAKE PLACID?

Elijah and Rebecca Bennett settled in Lake Placid when he was 46 years old and she was 38. Born in Connecticut in 1754 and crippled in the Revolutionary War, Elijah had the use of only one arm. Despite his handicap and age, he was a farmer and blacksmith.

WHO WAS THE FIRST OBSERVER IN THE WHITEFACE MOUNTAIN FIRE TOWER?

Born in Hartford, Connecticut, Sam Cheetham grew up in Dublin, Ireland, and moved to Saranac Lake after he contracted tuberculosis. Cheetham was fascinated by Whiteface Mountain and vowed he would someday reach its peak, even though he was so weak he could only climb stairs on his hands and knees. But in the spring of 1915, having regained his health, he won the job as first fire tower observer on his favorite mountain. On June 6, with a pack on his back, he made the six-and-a-half mile climb to the summit.

WHO WAS THE FIRST PERMANENT RESIDENT OF HAMILTON COUNTY?

An Abenaki Indian from Canada, Sabael Benedict left Quebec in 1767, made his way to Lake Champlain, built a birchbark canoe and paddled to New York State. He settled on the shore of Indian Lake near the present community of Sabael and married the daughter of a Dutch settler. The couple had three daughters and a son named Lewis Elijah, for whom Lewey Lake was named. When Benedict's wife died, he sewed her remains in birchbark and buried her on the banks of a little brook, now called Squaw Brook in her memory. Benedict's own death is shrouded in mystery. At the age of 108 he suddenly disappeared, and his body was never found.

WHO WAS THE FIRST WHITE MAN TO TREK THROUGH THE ADIRONDACKS?

In May of 1776, after the outbreak of the Revolution, Sir John Johnson of Johnstown and a number of his Tory friends headed north toward Canada. Their route took them through what is now the Raquette and Long Lake regions to the St. Lawrence River and Montreal. The party started its journey on snowshoes but later discarded them on the shore of a lake and continued by canoe. The pile of snowshoes (raquettes, in French) was discovered by local settlers, and Raquette Lake was named.

WHO WAS THE FIRST SETTLER OF LYON MOUNTAIN?

The highest peak in Clinton County, Lyon Mountain was called "Lion" on early maps, probably because it is shaped like a lion couchant. Oddly enough, the first person to settle on its slope was Nathaniel Lyon, a Vermonter who came to Plattsburgh in 1803. Traveling by ox cart up the frozen Saranac River, Lyon and his family stayed in Saranac village for a time before moving to the mountain that already bore his name. His granddaughter, Hattie Lyon, is credited with being the first woman to ascend this peak.

WHO WAS THE FIRST ITINERANT MINISTER IN THE SOUTHERN ADIRONDACKS?

Reverend Elisha Yale arrived in the region in 1804 and, at the age of 24, became pastor of the Presbyterian Church in Kingsboro (now Gloversville). Yale traveled north to preach the gospel in Wells and Lake Pleasant and set up missionary and Bible societies in outlying districts of the southern Adirondacks.

WHO WAS THE FIRST ADIRONDACKER TO BECOME A BASEBALL HERO?

When he was only 23 years old, Mineville's Johnny Podres -- the son of an iron ore miner -- pitched the Brooklyn Dodgers to a victory over the New York Yankees, making his team the winner of the 1955 World Series. Podres returned to Mineville in October. He was honored by a cheering crowd of 5,000 fans who gathered at Linney Field to pay their respects to the home town boy whose childhood nickname had been "Elmer the Great."

WHO WAS THE FIRST FORMER KING TO PURCHASE LAND IN THE ADIRONDACKS?

Napoleon's older brother, Joseph Bonaparte, driven out of Spain after serving as king for five years, bought more than 160,000 acres of Adirondack land. He hoped to set up an empire called "New France" for his brother, who was being held prisoner after losing the Battle of Waterloo, but the Emperor Napoleon died in captivity. In 1828, Joseph Bonaparte had a log fortress constructed at Natural Bridge and built a lodge at the end of the lake now called Lake Bonaparte.

WHO WAS THE FIRST PERMANENT JEWISH SETTLER IN THE ADIRONDACK REGION?

Nathan Littauer settled in Gloversville, just south of the Blue Line, in 1855, when he was only 25 years old. One year later he married Harriet Sporborg from Albany. Although Jewish peddlers often visited the Adirondacks, the Littauers were the first permanent residents. An immigrant from Breslau, Nathan first went to Albany, where he considered settling, but moved instead to Fulton County. He started out as a peddler and finally found success as a manufacturer of leather gloves. His first-born son, Lucius Littauer, went to Harvard, where he roomed with Teddy Roosevelt and became the first football coach in the school's history. Lucius later became a Congressman, serving five terms.

WHO WAS THE FIRST MEMBER OF THE HAND FAMILY TO SETTLE IN THE ADIRONDACKS?

In 1830, one year after moving from Vermont to Crown Point, Judge Augustus C. Hand was appointed Essex County Surrogate. Resettling in the county seat at Elizabethtown, he built the stately red brick house known as "Hand House." Judge Hand, a Democrat, served one term in Congress. He became a New York State Senator in 1844 and was named a justice of the State Supreme Court eight years later. Hand's grandson, Augustus Noble Hand, was born in Elizabethtown in 1869. Both he and his cousin, Learned Hand, became illustrious federal court judges. In fact, Learned Hand, who spent many summers at Hand House, was called "the most distinguished living English-speaking jurist."

WHO WAS THE FIRST WOMAN SENTENCED TO THE ELECTRIC CHAIR IN NEW YORK STATE?

On a rainy day in March 1925, Henry Soper was shot twice in the head while sleeping in his home in Essex. Two days later his wife was arrested and charged with the crime. Tried and convicted of first degree murder, Fanny Soper became the first woman in New York State to be sentenced to die in the electric chair. But Fanny was granted another trial and was given a 20-year sentence, serving part of it in Auburn Prison. The "Sphinx Woman," as she was called by the press, denied her guilt until she died in 1945 at the age of 67.

WHO BROUGHT THE FIRST FOUR-MAN BOBSLED TO LAKE PLACID?

In 1911, Count Ernest des Baillets of Belgium brought his four-man bobsled -- the first ever seen in the United States -- to Lake Placid. Unable to find anyone to build him a bobsled run, the disappointed Count went on to St. Agathe in Canada's Laurentians where a run was constructed. In 1920 he returned to Lake Placid and helped to found the pioneer winter sports club, the Sno Birds.

WHO WAS THE FIRST WOMAN HUNTING GUIDE IN NEW YORK STATE?

Julia Burton, born in a log cabin at Piseco Lake in 1896, was taught to shoot at the age of 14 by her father, a lumberjack. In 1912 Burton married Charlie W. Preston, the son of the owner of the Hosley House, a hotel in Wells. She began guiding hunting parties two years later, charging $10 a day. The first licensed woman hunting guide in the state, Burton lived to be 73 years old.

WHO WAS THE FIRST BLACK GOLF PRO IN THE ADIRONDACKS?

In 1947, the old Cedar River House in Indian Lake, which had its own nine-hole golf course, was sold to Dewey Brown, who owned and operated the resort for the next 25 years. Brown, possibly the first African-American member of the P.G.A., was well known for his hand-made golf clubs; President Harding was one of his customers. Because of his gentle and sincere manner, sportswriters called Brown the "Knight of the Fairways."

WHO WAS THE FIRST ESSEX COUNTY JUDGE?

Daniel Ross, the first attorney in the town of Essex, lived in that community from 1784 until his death in 1847. Ross, who was elected the first Essex County Judge in November 1800, was married to William Gilliland's daughter, Elizabeth, after whom Elizabethtown, the Essex County seat, was named.

WHO WAS THE FIRST ADIRONDACK STRONG MAN?

Known as the "Lewis Giant," Joe Call first revealed his strength during the War of 1812, when he performed such feats as lifting a one-ton cannon and serving cider to the troops from a huge barrel balanced on his shoulder. Just after the war, Call, who was barely six feet tall and weighed less than 200 pounds, killed an abusive British grenadier with his bare hands. After touring the world billed as "Modern Hercules," Call returned to Lewis in 1834 and died from a carbuncle on his neck.

WHO WAS THE FIRST "FIRST LADY" TO RIDE A BOBSLED?

During the 1932 Winter Olympic Games in Lake Placid, the daring First Lady, Eleanor Roosevelt, took a ride on a bobsled at Mt. Van Hoevenberg.

WHO WAS THE FIRST WINTER FORTY-SIXER?

On March 10, 1962, Edgar B. Bean reached the summit of Blake Peak and became the first person to climb all 46 high peaks in winter.

WHAT

WHAT WAS THE FIRST "WATCHDOG OF THE ADIRONDACKS"?

On January 3, 1902, the Association for the Protection of the Adirondacks was formed by Warren Higley, president of the Adirondack League Club. Higley was once described by a colleague as "fine-looking, knew something about the Adirondacks and forestry, but had no brains." Since its membership was drawn largely from private clubs and preserves, the Association, which still exists, was charged with representing only the interests of the rich. The group soon earned a reputation as the "Watchdog of the Adirondacks."

WHAT WAS THE VERDICT IN THE FIRST ADIRONDACK GANGSTER TRIAL?

Dutch Schultz, a notorious beer bootlegger whose real name was Arthur Flegenheimer, was tried in the Franklin County Courthouse in Malone for evading $92,000 in taxes on illicit income of $481,000. Local residents were fascinated to learn that, some years earlier, the gangster had served as a Long Lake deputy sheriff for about six months. Schultz's trial began on July 23, 1935, and ended on August 1, when the jury of farmers delivered its verdict -- not guilty. Two months later, Dutch Schultz died the day after he was struck by a barrage of machine-gun fire at the Palace Chop House and Tavern in New Jersey.

WHAT IS THE NAME OF THE FIRST ADIRONDACK MARCHING BAND?

According to village historians, the Cambridge Marching Band, whose roots go back to 1853, is the first independent military-style band in the country. Although this claim is debatable, the Cambridge ensemble is certainly the first military style marching band in the Adirondacks and has continued playing -- and marching -- since its inception, with a little time off for World War II. For a short period in 1869, the band divided into two separate groups after a dispute over who would play first cornet.

WHAT IS THE NAME OF THE FIRST TEENAGER TO HAVE A HIGH PEAK NAMED AFTER HER?

In 1839, Esther McComb headed out alone to climb Whiteface Mountain, but when she reached the top of another mountain she realized she was lost. The fifteen-year-old spent the night on the peak before a search party found her the next day, and the 4,297-foot mountain that the girl mistakenly conquered was named Mt. Esther in her honor. One hundred years later, a plaque was installed at Mt. Esther's summit, commemorating the girl who had ascended the peak for the "sheer joy of climbing."

WHAT IS THE TITLE OF THE FIRST POPULAR BOOK OF TRAVEL IN THE ADIRONDACKS?

Published in England in 1839, "Wild Scenes in the Forest" was an account by Charles Fenno Hoffman of his trip, accompanied by the guide John Cheney, into the mountains. He told of seeing bears and wild gorges and of hearing complaints that the Adirondacks were being spoiled by visitors. This intrepid traveler attempted to climb Mt. Marcy despite the fact that he had only one leg. When he failed in his attempt, he broke down and sobbed.

WHAT IS THE NAME OF THE FIRST THEME PARK IN THE COUNTRY?

In 1948, Arto Monaco, a former cartoonist for Walt Disney, MGM, and Warner Brothers, returned to his hometown of Upper Jay and designed "Santa's Workshop," which became the first theme park in the United States. Located in Wilmington, the park contains a children's village of log houses with a Mother Goose motif, a "North Pole" that stays frozen all year round, Santa's home and workshop, and Santa himself along with his elves. Monaco later created a second park, the "Land of Makebelieve," on 85 acres of land along the Ausable River in Upper Jay. This creation opened in 1954, a year before Disneyland.

WHAT WAS THE SITE OF THE FIRST SUSPENSION BRIDGE ACROSS THE HUDSON?

Just south of North Creek, at Washburn's Eddy, Robert Cogdell Gilchrist built the first suspension bridge to cross the Hudson River. Gilchrist, a Confederate Army major who moved to the Adirondacks after the Civil War, opened his bridge on September 8, 1871. Fifteen feet wide with a 230-foot span, the bridge soared twenty-five feet above the water. Today the only evidence of Gilchrist's bridge are the abutments and cables; no one knows when or why the bridge went down.

WHAT WAS THE FIRST RECORDED ICE FISHING CATCH?

The first statistics of winter ice fishing on Lake Champlain, which were recorded in 1894, show that 33,170 pounds of fish were caught on the New York side of the lake.

WHAT WAS THE FIRST LEGAL EFFORT TO PRESERVE THE ADIRONDACK FORESTS?

The New York State Legislature made its first attempt to preserve the forests of the Adirondacks in 1808, when the lawmakers approved a measure making it a misdemeanor to cut down or destroy the "public woods in the county of Essex."

WHAT WAS THE FIRST FORESTRY COLLEGE IN NORTH AMERICA?

In 1898, on 30,000 acres of land at Axton near Upper Saranac Lake, the New York State College of Forestry, administered by Cornell University, held its first class. The school, with only four students its first year, was directed by Bernhard Fernow, a forester from Germany. Five years later, when the enrollment had grown to 70, the school was closed by the governor in response to complaints from summer residents who charged that the students were making noise and causing fire danger and aesthetic damage.

ON WHAT MAP DID MT. MARCY FIRST APPEAR BY NAME?

In the second edition of Barr's Atlas of New York State, published in 1839, Mt. Marcy made its first appearance on a map of the region.

WHAT WAS THE NAME OF THE FIRST TUBERCULOSIS PATIENT TO TAKE THE CURE IN SARANAC LAKE?

During the winter of 1874, Edward C. Edgar, Saranac Lake's first recorded tuberculosis patient, stayed at the home of a guide named Lucius Evans while taking the cure.

WHAT WAS THE NAME OF THE FIRST WHITE CHILD BORN IN KEENE VALLEY?

Benjamin Payne, the first permanent resident of Keene Valley, arrived from Westport in 1797 by following marked trees and hauling his goods in a "jumper" -- a primitive carrier made of two long poles. Payne settled in the valley with his wife, who gave birth to a daughter, Betsey Payne, in 1798.

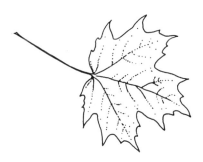

WHAT WAS THE FIRST MAGAZINE DEVOTED TO THE ADIRONDACKS?

Harry V. Radford, an 18-year-old from New York City who had spent many summers with his mother in the Adirondacks, started a quarterly publication, Woods and Water, in 1898. Circulation soon reached 20,000 readers. Radford used his magazine to crusade for the restoration of the moose and beaver, and to lobby for laws to protect the black bear. Setting his sights farther than the Adirondacks, Radford headed for Labrador and the Pacific Northwest. It was on an expedition up the MacKenzie River to Hudson's Bay and the Arctic Circle that Radford met a tragic end. In 1914, word reached the Adirondacks that the explorer had been murdered by an Eskimo.

WHAT GEAR WAS USED FOR THE FIRST WINTER ASCENT OF MT. MARCY?

In March of 1893, wearing snowshoes, two employees of the Adirondack Mountain Reserve, Benjamin Pond and J. Wesley Otis, made the first winter ascent of the highest peak in the Adirondacks.

WHAT WAS THE TITLE OF THE FIRST ADIRONDACK NOVEL?

Published in 1852, "The Forest," by Jedidiah Vincent Huntington, who had recently converted to Roman Catholicism, was a romance that combined the spiritual and the secular. Set in the forests of the Adirondacks, the novel used hunting and fishing at Lewey Lake and Lake Pleasant as background.

WHAT WAS THE NAME OF THE FIRST IRON MINE IN THE ADIRONDACKS?

Ore from the Cheever mine just north of Port Henry was removed as early as 1766, and was taken by boat to Major Philip Skene's settlement, now Whitehall, on the head of Lake Champlain. Some historians have claimed that, by order of Benedict Arnold, ore from this mine was made into iron for ships later engaged in Revolutionary War battles.

WHAT WAS THE PURPOSE OF THE FIRST ADIRONDACK CLUB FOR LUMBERJACKS?

In response to concerns about alcohol consumption by loggers when they went into town on their days off, a club for lumberjacks was proposed in the summer of 1942. The crew at Clarence Strife's camp near Bisby Lake was the first to sign up, and others soon followed. The Woodsmen's Club, the first created especially for lumberjacks, had its grand opening on March 11, 1943, in a large house that had been purchased in Forestport. Guests enjoyed a sumptuous meal prepared by a camp cook, Sam LeMay, with the help of some Forestport ladies. In an effort to keep its members out of bars, the club offered rooms, showers, food and recreation. Most guests arrived sober, but some, having first stopped in town to toss down a few drinks, had to be put to bed.

WHAT HOTEL WAS THE FIRST IN THE WORLD TO BE LIT WITH ELECTRIC LIGHTS?

Considered by some to be the finest hotel in the United States, The Prospect House in Blue Mountain Lake opened its doors in 1882. Each of the 300 guest rooms had running water and, for the first time in history, electric lights. The electricity was generated by two dynamos fueled by a wood fire. The owner of the hotel, Frederick Durant, employed a wine steward, hired black waiters, and served his guests turtle soup. The Prospect House also had a steam elevator, a two-story outhouse, a bowling alley, and steam heat. The rates were $25 a week in summer; in off-season they were dropped to $15.

WHAT WAS THE ROUTE OF THE FIRST RECORDED CAMPING TRIP THROUGH THE ADIRONDACKS BY A WOMAN TOURIST?

In 1855, the Hon. Amelia M. Murray, 60, a maid-of-honor to Queen Victoria, accompanied by the governor of New York, Horatio Seymour, his niece, and three guides, embarked on a camping trip through the region. The plucky Englishwoman traveled by buckboard, canoe and foot from Elizabethtown to Saranac Lake and on to Stony Creek, Raquette Lake and Boonville. In her hamper, Ms. Murray carried biscuits, arrowroot and dried soup. Legend has it that she introduced the use of lemon with tea to Adirondack guides, a custom they soon adopted. After completing the last leg of the arduous journey, Murray spent three days recovering in a Utica hotel.

WHAT WAS THE FIRST NEWSPAPER PUBLISHED IN ESSEX COUNTY?

In 1810, Luther Marsh began publication of The Reveille, a weekly newspaper published in Elizabethtown. The yearly subscription rate was $2, half paid in advance. Edited by Ezra Carter Gross and William Ray, The Reveille struggled along for several years until it ceased publication in 1814. Gross, a lawyer, went on to represent his district in Congress and Ray became a writer of turgid histories.

WHAT BOOK FIRST DREW ATTENTION TO THE HEALTH BENEFITS OF LIVING IN THE ADIRONDACKS?

Reverend Joel T. Headley was forced to leave his job at the New York Tribune due to an "overwrought brain." He moved to the Adirondacks and wrote a book called "The Adirondacks, or Life in the Woods." Published in 1846, it credited the climate of the Adirondack Mountains with effecting the clergyman's cure. Headley was one of the most widely read authors of his day, but his florid style caused Edgar Allen Poe to call him "the autocrat of all quacks."

WHAT WAS THE NAME OF THE FIRST METHODIST PREACHER TO VISIT ESSEX COUNTY?

Thrown out of his Massachusetts home when his parents discovered he had embraced the Methodist faith, Richard Jacobs became an itinerant preacher. With his young wife, he toured through Northern New York in 1796, traveling as far as Essex and Clinton counties. On his way home, Jacobs tried to ford the Schroon River on horseback and drowned. His parents, grieved by the loss of their son, converted to Methodism.

WHAT WAS THE FIRST STEAMBOAT TO SAIL ON AN ADIRONDACK LAKE?

In about 1800 the steamboat "Mattie," carried on a wagon pulled by four horses, was transported to Lake Placid, where it was used to sail tourists around the lake for a charge of $1. The owner, Theodore White, soon dismantled the boat and replaced it with another, the "Lillie," which was torched by arsonists. Local rowboat operators, who had charged $3 for the trip, were delighted.

WHAT WERE THE NAMES OF THE FIRST TWO ESSEX COUNTY RESIDENTS TO ENLIST IN THE CIVIL WAR?

In April 1861, Washington Irving Sawyer and Napoleon Joubert, both from Westport, enlisted to fight in the Union Army. Sawyer was killed in June of the next year in the battle of Gaines' Mill in Virginia. Joubert was wounded in the fighting but recovered and lived until 1901.

WHAT WAS THE FIRST NORTH-SOUTH HIGHWAY IN THE ADIRONDACKS?

Laid out in 1790 from Washington County to the Canadian border, Rogers Old Road was the first highway built in the Adirondacks that ran from north to south. Following what is now Route 9, it cost $16 a mile to construct.

WHAT WAS THE FIRST LAW CURBING THE KILLING OF DEER?

In 1705, a law forbidding the hunting of deer between August 1 and January 1 was passed, effectively creating the first hunting season.

WHAT WAS THE NAME OF THE FIRST HOTEL ON LAKE GEORGE?

Opened in 1800, the Mohican House at Bolton Landing served guests traveling from Saratoga Springs and catered to "artists and people of culture." The hotel, with accomodations for 90 guests, charged $15 a week or $3 a day. It closed its doors in 1889.

WHAT WAS THE NAME OF THE FIRST FEMALE TRAVEL WRITER TO VISIT AND THEN WRITE ABOUT THE ADIRONDACKS?

Completely deaf and without a sense of taste or smell, the famous British authoress Harriet Martineau headed north from Saratoga, which she disliked, into the Adirondacks. She published a detailed account of her travels in London in 1838, writing: "What a wealth of beauty is there for future residents yet unborn."

WHAT WERE THE EFFECTS OF THE FIRST RECORDED TORNADO IN THE ADIRONDACKS?

On September 20, 1845, a tornado appeared over Lake Ontario and headed toward the Adirondacks. After crossing the Oswegatchie River, the twister removed a frame schoolhouse from its foundation, leaving the students and their teacher unharmed. In the Franklin County community of Derrick, the tornado resulted in thousands of acres of blown-down timber and two place names -- Windfall House and Windfall Pond. A storm of hail followed the twister; some hailstones, which were as big as hen's eggs, caused serious injuries to cattle as they fell.

WHAT WAS THE NAME OF THE FIRST CANINE FORTY-SIXER?

Chrissie Wendell, a white mutt with black spots on his face who belonged to a clergyman's family, climbed Sawtooth Mountain in 1948, making him the first dog to scale all 46 Adirondack high peaks. Years later, when Chrissie had become old and sickly, the Wendells were forced to have him put to sleep. They carried his body to the top of Mount Jo and buried him with his nose pointing west toward the high peaks he had conquered.

WHAT WAS THE FIRST TRAIN TO RUN COMPLETELY THROUGH THE ADIRONDACKS?

In November of 1875, the D&H Railroad completed its line between New York and Canada. Hundreds of workers had spent three years building the railroad through the rugged Adirondacks. Almost a century later, the D&H's passenger train, "The Laurentian," made its final trip along the shores of Lake Champlain.

WHAT WAS THE FIRST NAME GIVEN TO LAKE GEORGE?

Father Isaac Jogues, a Jesuit missionary who was trying to convert Iroquois Indians to Christianity, was captured in 1642 and taken south into the Lake Champlain valley, where he was tortured. Perhaps it was during this voyage that Jogues first saw Lake George, which he named "Lac du Saint Sacrement." The Jesuit priest spent three years in France recovering from his ordeal, returned to Quebec to continue his missionary work, and was killed in 1646.

WHAT WAS THE SITE OF THE FIRST WINTER CARNIVAL AND ICE PALACE IN AMERICA?

In 1898, a Saranac Lake organization called The Pontiac Club, chaired by Dr. Edward Trudeau, decided to organize a mid-winter carnival featuring games, contests, winter sports and a parade. That year, the queen of the carnival, Hazel Fowler, reigned in a palace made completely of ice. Fifty feet high and with a facade 150 feet long, the ice palace cost $500 to build. The winter carnival -- complete with palaces featuring ice-carved rooms, stairways and turrets -- continues to be a Saranac Lake tradition.

WHAT COLOR WAS THE FIRST STEAMBOAT TO SAIL THE LENGTH OF LAKE CHAMPLAIN?

In 1809, the steamer "Vermont," 120 feet long, 20 feet wide and painted black, began running the length of Lake Champlain. The craft reached a top speed of four miles an hour when the wind was blowing in the right direction. Built by John and James Winans in 1808 after they had worked with Robert Fulton on the "Clermont," the "Vermont" was the second steamboat in the world to operate successfully as a commercial vessel.

100

WHAT GOVERNOR RODE THE FIRST CHAIRLIFT UP WHITEFACE MOUNTAIN?

During the dedication ceremony in 1958, Averell Harriman, then governor of New York State, rode the first chairlift up Whiteface Mountain. Unfortunately the chairlift broke down, leaving the governor suspended in mid-air for an hour and a half.

WHAT WAS THE FIRST ADIRONDACK LAKE TO BE "FISHED OUT"?

As early as 1820, conservationists decried overfishing when the last trout was taken from Saranac Lake.

WHAT WAS THE FIRST TOWN IN HAMILTON COUNTY?

On April 1, 1805, the male inhabitants of the settlements of Wells and Lake Pleasant met at the home of Moses Craig and formed the Town of Wells, the first town within the boundaries of what is now Hamilton County.

WHAT ADIRONDACK GROUP MADE THE FIRST BAKER'S PEELS?

A community of Shakers settled in the town of Arietta in the early 1800's and began producing products made of wood -- furniture, barrel staves and bowls, as well as baker's "peels," which were flat paddles with long handles used to remove bread from ovens. By 1820 the Shakers had left the Adirondacks, but the manufacture of peels continued for years throughout the region.

WHAT WAS THE HOME OF THE FIRST DOCTOR TO PRACTICE HOMEOPATHY IN THE ADIRONDACKS?

E. Darwin Jones of Keeseville graduated from Albany Medical College in 1844. He practiced homeopathic medicine for several years in Clinton County before moving to Albany.

WHAT WAS THE HOME OF THE FIRST AMERICAN OLYMPIC GOLD MEDALIST?

On January 26, 1924, in Chamonix, France, a young Lake Placid resident named Charles Jewtraw skated in the first event of what would become the first Olympic Winter Games. Jewtraw amazed onlookers by winning the 500-meter speedskating race and becoming the first American ever to bring home an Olympic gold medal for winter sports.

WHAT WAS THE FIRST NAME GIVEN TO MT. COLVIN?

In the early 1870's, a Keene Valley guide named Orson "Old Mountain" Phelps called this peak Sabael, after Sabael Benedict, an Abenaki from Indian Lake. It was later proposed that the mountain be named after Verplanck Colvin, who had made the first recorded ascent of the peak in August 1873, and Phelps agreed. Several years later, an unsuccessful attempt to change the name back to Sabael was fueled by an argument between Colvin and the artist Roswell Shurtleff over which man had killed a deer at Upper Ausable Lake.

WHEN

WHEN WAS THE FIRST GREAT ADIRONDACK FOREST FIRE?

From April 20 to June 8, 1903, forest fires destroyed more than 600,000 acres of Adirondack timberland. An unusually dry winter and spring had left piles of dead tree limbs and brush extremely susceptible to fire, and many blazes broke out along railroad lines as cinders were discharged from locomotives. Around Elizabethtown and Keene Valley, 17,000 acres were burned and nearly every tree was killed. Among the many losses was the Adirondack Lodge, a rustic hotel, which was completely destroyed. Several days of drenching rains finally extinguished the flames.

WHEN WERE LEAN-TOS FIRST PERMITTED IN THE ADIRONDACKS?

In 1913, the state Conservation Commission adopted regulations permitting the construction of three-sided open camps on specific wilderness sites. These rustic shelters became known as Adirondack lean-tos and, no matter who constructed them, were considered state property for the use of all campers and hikers.

WHEN WAS ADIRONDACK MURRAY'S FIRST VISIT?

William H.H. Murray, a Connecticut clergyman who became known as "Adirondack Murray," first visited the region in 1864. He described his trip in an article he wrote for the Meriden Literary Recorder which he later expanded into a book called "Adventures in the Wilderness; or, Camp-life in the Adirondacks," published in 1869. The book unleashed a flood of tourists into the Adirondack region, causing a phenomenon called the "Murray Rush".

WHEN WAS THE FIRST ADIRONDACK TRAIL GUIDE PUBLISHED?

In 1934, the Adirondack Mountain Club published "Guide to Adirondack Trails," written by Dr. Orra Phelps. Her book was the first trail guide to the Adirondacks, and became the prototype of a series of guides published by the club. A teacher and naturalist as well as a doctor, Phelps was a school physician in Herkimer County and a Navy lieutenant in World War II before becoming a staff doctor at the Albany veterans' hospital, where she stayed until her retirement.

WHEN WAS THE FIRST RECORDED EARTHQUAKE IN THE ADIRONDACKS?

Verplanck Colvin, the superintendent of the Adirondack Survey, recorded an earthquake on February 9, 1876, at Saranac Lake. This was the first written record of such an event in the Adirondacks.

WHEN DID THE FIRST EUROPEAN EXPLORER VIEW THE ADIRONDACKS?

Jacques Cartier, a French navigator and explorer, sailed up the St. Lawrence River in 1535 and, from a peak that he named Mount Royal, near what is now Montreal, looked southward and saw the Adirondack Mountains.

113

WHEN WAS THE FIRST ASCENT OF A HIGH PEAK?

On June 2, 1797, Charles Broadhead climbed the 4,626-foot Giant Mountain while he was surveying the south boundary of the Old Military Tract. This was the first recorded ascent of an Adirondack peak taller than 4,000 feet.

WHEN WAS THE FIRST FOREST MANAGEMENT PLAN CREATED?

William Seward Webb, a railroad builder and lumbering tycoon, bought 143,494 acres of land in northern Herkimer and Hamilton counties in 1890. Webb called his estate Nehasene, and constructed a sprawling lodge overlooking a body of water that he named Lila Lake in honor of his wife. Webb hired the famous forester Gifford Pinchot to help him use his vast acreage to demonstrate a range of conservation practices, thus creating the first scientific forest management plan for private lands in U.S. history.

WHEN WAS PAPER FIRST MADE IN THE ADIRONDACKS?

A small mill was established on the upper Hudson River in 1866 that made paper from ground poplar. But a year later, after chemicals had replaced grinders for making wood pulp, mill owners discovered that spruce was the best wood for paper making. This discovery led to the vast lumbering of giant virgin spruce trees in the Adirondacks.

WHEN DID FREUD FIRST VISIT THE ADIRONDACKS?

Sigmund Freud, the world's first psychoanalyst, and his colleague, C.G. Jung, visited Keene Valley in September 1909 and spent three days at Putnam Camp. In a letter to his family describing the log cabin in which he stayed, Freud wrote: "Everything is left very rough and primitive but it comes off. Mixing bowls serve as wash bowls, china mugs for glasses, etc....We have discovered that there are special books on camping in which instruction is given about all this primitive equipment."

WHEN WAS THE FIRST ADIRONDACK BIKING CLUB ORGANIZED?

The Keene Valley Bicycle Club was formed in 1897. Its members constructed and maintained a bike path between St. Huberts and Keene Valley that was a popular route to the base of the High Peaks. By 1920 the club had disbanded and its trails were being used by hikers.

WHEN DID THE BLUE LINE FIRST APPEAR ON MAPS?

A law was passed in 1892 establishing a 2-million-acre Adirondack Park, the boundaries of which were delineated on a map by a blue line. Since then, official state maps use a blue line to show the boundary of the Adirondack Park, and the term, "within the Blue Line," has become common.

WHEN WAS THE NAME "ADIRONDACK" FIRST USED?

In 1837 Ebenezer Emmons, the chief geologist of the first state topographical survey of the region, wrote: "The cluster of mountains in the neighborhood of the Upper Hudson and Ausable Rivers I propose to call the Adirondack Group, a name by which a well-known tribe of Indians who once hunted there may be commemorated." The origin of the name is uncertain, but some believe it was taken from "ratirontaks," meaning "those who eat trees," a pejorative Iroquois name for the Algonquins, who supposedly were reduced to living on tree buds and bark in winter.

WHEN WERE HOPS FIRST GROWN IN THE ADIRONDACKS?

Commercial hop production began in Franklin County in 1825, and the region became the most productive hop-growing area outside of the Mohawk Valley. By 1880, when the hop industry was near its peak, Franklin County produced more than 1 million pounds of the crop.

WHEN WAS THE FIRST MAGAZINE ARTICLE ON THE ADIRONDACKS PUBLISHED?

An article entitled "Some Accounts of the Two Visits to the Mountains in Essex County, New York, in the Years 1836 and 1837; With a Sketch of the Northern Sources of the Hudson" appeared in Family Magazine in 1838. The author was William C. Redfield, an esteemed meteorologist, who visited the region at the invitation of a mine-owner named David Henderson.

WHEN WAS THE FIRST RELEASE OF A YUKON LYNX INTO THE ADIRONDACKS?

By the turn of the century, excessive logging had destroyed the habitat of the Adirondack lynx, and the animal had all but vanished from the region. In an effort to restore the lynx population, 18 of these animals captured in the Yukon territory were set free in 1989 by the Adirondack Wildlife Program in Newcomb. From January to May of the next year, 40 more of the felines were released.

WHEN DID THE ADIRONDACK REGION FIRST APPEAR ON A MAP?

The "Theatrum Orbis Terrarum," drawn by Abraham Ortelius, geographer to King Philip II of Spain, contains a map of 'New France' that shows the area of Northern New York State and calls it Avacal. This series of fifty-three maps was published in 1570.

WHEN DID CONSTRUCTION START ON THE FIRST HIGHWAY INTO THE ADIRONDACK INTERIOR?

In 1810, the Northwest Bay Road was started. Still in use today, the road was constructed from Westport to Elizabethtown and then across parts of Franklin and St. Lawrence counties to provide a route from Lake Champlain to the settlements along the St. Lawrence.

WHEN DID THE FIRST PERMANENT PHYSICIAN ARRIVE IN THE ADIRONDACKS?

Dr. Asa Post moved from Vermont to Elizabethtown in 1792 at the age of 27 to cure his own consumption. After serving as the local doctor for several years, he left medicine to become a farmer.

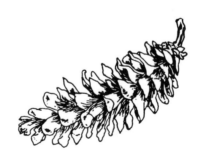

WHEN WAS THE FIRST ELECTROCUTION AT DANNEMORA PRISON?

Cal Wood shot and killed his father-in-law, Leander Pasco, on a rainy May day in Stony Creek by firing 10 shots into the victim's body. Wood had several grievances against the older man, whom he claimed had removed nuts from his wagon wheels, robbed him of potatoes, and destroyed a goose nest in which two geese were sitting on their eggs. While detained in a cell in the Lake George jail, Wood was tried and convicted twice. Finally, on August 2, 1892, he became the first person to die in the electric chair at the maximum security prison in Dannemora.

WHEN WAS THE FIRST ADIRONDACK SCHOOL DISTRICT FORMED?

The first Adirondack public school district, in Keene Valley, was formed at a meeting of its first trustees in 1813. For several years classes were held in private homes. In 1817, for example, the district voted "to give Luther Walker one dollar and 25 cents for use of his room to keep school this winter." Although it was seven years before the district got its first schoolhouse, construction of the building took only one week and cost $168 for materials and labor.

WHEN DID THE FIRST AMERICAN INDIAN ATTEMPT TO VOTE IN HAMILTON COUNTY?

Mitchell Sabattis, an expert guide who played the violin, tried to vote in Long Lake in 1862. He was challenged by Isaac B. C. Robinson "on the ground of his being an Indian and the Legislature not having power to make him a voter." Not dissuaded from becoming politically involved, Sabattis, an Abenaki Indian, was named Long Lake's Commissioner of Highways in 1866.

WHEN WAS "CHAMP" FIRST SIGHTED?

The Lake Champlain monster, known today as "Champ," was first seen by Samuel de Champlain in July of 1609. Champlain reported that he had spotted a serpent-like creature 20 feet long, thick as a barrel, "with a head that resembled that of a horse."

WHEN DID THE FIRST AIRPLANE LAND IN THE ADIRONDACKS?

George A. Gray of Boston took off from the North Country village of Malone in his Burgess-Wright biplane on October 13, 1912. Encountering high winds while flying over Whiteface Mountain, he was forced to land in a wheatfield on Fletcher's Farm northeast of Bloomingdale. The pioneer pilot was soon able to continue his flight to Saranac Lake, where he landed on the race track. For several days he delivered packages and took passengers for short trips. One of these thrill-seekers was a Miss Edith M. Stearns. George and young Edith fell in love and were married a year later.

WHEN WAS IRON ORE FIRST MINED IN SUBSTANTIAL AMOUNTS IN MINEVILLE?

In 1804, open pit mining operations began in Mineville. Soon tunnels had to be dug to remove the valuable iron ore and, by 1852, hundreds of tunnels, some as deep as 300 feet, had been excavated. By 1905, 13 million tons of ore had been removed.

WHEN WAS THE FIRST STUDY OF THE ADIRONDACK BLACK FLY COMPLETED?

The State Entomologist's Office of the New York State Museum finished the first study of this famous pest in 1900.

WHEN WAS THE FIRST STOCKING OF AN ADIRONDACK LAKE?

New York Governor Horatio Seymour ordered bass put into Adirondack waters in 1862 in response to complaints about the declining numbers of fish.

WHEN WAS SOURCE OF THE HUDSON FIRST NAMED?

When the surveyor Verplanck Colvin discovered the tiny pond on the southwest slope of Mt. Marcy in 1872, he called it "a minute, unpretending tear of the clouds." Eventually, Lake Tear-of-the-Clouds became the official name of the source of the Hudson.

WHEN WAS THE NAME SARANAC FIRST USED?

In a timber report dated 1745, the name Saranac, allegedly meaning "The Lake of the Falling Stars," was given to the river that comes out of the Adirondacks, flows through Plattsburgh, and empties into Lake Champlain.

135

WHEN WAS THE FIRST SURVEY DONE IN THE ADIRONDACKS?

In 1771, Archibald Campbell, assisted by eight American Indians, subdivided the Totten and Crossfield Purchase into 50 lots. The survey, which was accomplished by long-distance sighting, was the basis for many lawsuits. After the Revolution began, the land reverted back to the People of New York.

WHEN DID THE FIRST VEHICLE ENTER THE WHITEFACE MOUNTAIN HIGHWAY?

Although vigorously opposed by conservationists, construction of the highway up 4,865-foot Whiteface Mountain began on Christmas Day, 1931. The road was opened to traffic on July 20, 1935, and the first vehicle to pass through the gate was a 50-year-old horse-drawn stagecoach that had once carried mail and passengers between Paul Smiths and Port Kent. In September, President Franklin Delano Roosevelt dedicated the highway as a memorial to New York State's World War I dead.

WHEN WAS THE ADIRONDACK MOUNTAIN CLUB STARTED?

The club, commonly known as ADK, is a nonprofit organization appealing to mountain climbers and hikers. Founded in 1922, its first general meeting took place at the Lake Placid Club.

WHEN WERE HORSE NAILS FIRST MADE BY MACHINE?

In 1856, Daniel Dodge invented a machine that automatically made horse nails. Seven years later Dodge formed the Ausable Horse Nail Company in Keeseville, bringing industry and jobs to the region.

WHEN WAS MAN-MADE SNOW FIRST USED IN THE OLYMPIC GAMES?

The Olympic Winter Games of 1980, held in Lake Placid, were the first to take advantage of the new snow-making technology. Using a technique that still exists, a combination of compressed air and pressurized water was shot out of a snow gun. Seven times denser than the natural material, man-made snow is more impervious to rain, thaw, and the effects of skis running over it.

WHEN DID THE FIRST STEAMBOAT SAIL ON LAKE GEORGE?

Built in 1816 with a brick smokestack and two long boilers, the "James Caldwell" was launched in 1817. It traveled at a speed of four miles an hour and took a whole day to sail from one end of the lake to the other. The craft came to an untimely end when it burned at its pier in 1820. Some felt the blaze was an "insurance fire."

WHEN WAS THE FIRST BRIDGE BUILT ACROSS AUSABLE CHASM?

One day in 1805, a cedar tree fell across Ausable Chasm and lodged just below the highest point on the east side of the deep crevice, bridging the gap for the first time. A pair of oxen was brought to one side of the chasm, but the yoke needed to link them into a team was on the other side. Balancing the ox-yoke on his shoulders, a daring observer named Captain Samuel Jackson marched across the fallen tree and delivered the yoke to the oxen, who were then used in the construction of the twelve-foot-wide bridge.

WHEN WERE LOG BRANDS FIRST USED ON THE RAQUETTE RIVER?

When loggers started using rivers to drive timber, it became necessary to stamp the ends of logs with company brands in order to keep track of ownership. The first brand in the Raquette River was registered in 1851; by 1900 there were 102 registered brands in such distinctive shapes as a star, double circle, figure eight and crow's foot. As lumbering became more mechanized, branding was no longer needed and in 1923 the last log brand was registered in St. Lawrence County.

WHEN WERE THE FIRST CCC CAMPS ESTABLISHED IN THE ADIRONDACKS?

A month after Franklin Delano Roosevelt's presidential inauguration in 1933, Congress passed a law creating the Civilian Conservation Corps (CCC), designed to provide employment for young men who could not find work during the Depression. In April of that year, the head of the New York State Conservation Department announced that there was enough work in the Adirondacks to keep at least 1,000 CCC enrollees employed. By May, CCC camps had been set up in Arietta, Tupper Lake, Fish Creek Pond, Wawbeek and Mountain Pond, and the workers were busy building trails, clearing roads and enlarging campsites.

WHEN WAS THE FIRST CROSSCUT SAW USED IN HAMILTON COUNTY?

Two loggers who worked with Frank Stanley in 1891 cutting timber on Kunjamuck Mountain in the Town of Lake Pleasant used the first crosscut saw ever seen in the region. With the traditional axe one man could cut an average of 70 logs a day, but by using the crosscut saw, two men could saw 160 logs in the same amount of time.

WHEN DID THE FIRST PERMANENT SETTLER COME TO BLUE MOUNTAIN LAKE?

Chauncey Hathorn, a Saratoga tailor, first visited Blue Mountain Lake in 1855 and spent the next winter at Eagle's Nest. In 1859, suffering from tuberculosis, Hathorn came back to stay and eventually recovered his health. He was said to be a man of education and breeding, fair in his dealings, something of a recluse, and a periodic drunk.

145

WHEN WAS THE FIRST PUBLIC EXECUTION IN CLINTON COUNTY?

John Dougherty, a soldier, was convicted in 1813 of the murder of John Wait, a resident of Salmon Falls. Dougherty was hanged on the Boynton Road near the shore of Lake Champlain.

WHEN WAS THE FIRST SCHOOL OPENED IN CROWN POINT?

Elisha Rhoades started a school in his Crown Point home in 1805. The first five students, taught by Mrs. Rhoades, sat on pine slabs set up in the same room where Rhoades also ran a small grocery store.

WHEN WAS THE FIRST NAVAL BATTLE OF THE REVOLUTION?

A battle between the English, under the command of Captain Pringle, and the Americans, under Benedict Arnold, took place on October 11, 1776, off the west shore of Valcour Island in Lake Champlain. Arnold and his troops fled during the night, sailing south, but the British overtook them two days later and vanquished them.

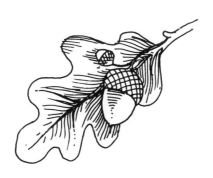

WHEN WAS THE FIRST RECORDED DISCOVERY OF WOLLASTONITE IN WILLSBORO?

In 1810, Dr. William Meade, a chemist and mineral collector, discovered evidence of a deposit of wollastonite while digging in the Willsboro area. Wollastonite, a naturally occuring calcium metasilicate, was named after an English chemist and minerologist, Henry Hyde Wollaston. The mineral is used in the manufacture of such products as tile, ceramics and paint, and might once have been an ingredient in Native American pottery.

WHEN WAS THE FIRST WEDDING IN THE TUPPER LAKE AREA?

In 1840, a man named Michael Cole cleared a patch of ground and built a cabin on the Raquette River. One of his daughters, Sarah, became the first bride in the region when she married Theodorus Westcott in 1850. The wedding was performed by a timber cruiser who was also a preacher. Since the man could only officiate legally in St. Lawrence County, the couple rowed to a small island on Big Tupper Lake, just over the county line, for the ceremony. The island become known as "Sally's Rock."

WHEN WAS GRAPHITE FIRST FOUND IN THE ADIRONDACKS?

Legend has it that Mrs. Zuba Pearl was driving her cows home along Grassy Hill in Ticonderoga when one animal slipped and pulled a piece of wet moss from a rock, revealing the lustrous graphite. Others say the mineral was first found by Charles Wood in 1815 while he was chasing his cattle. In any case, Guy C. Baldwin discovered a use for the graphite 15 years later when he invented a process for making large, solid, black lead pencils, a business he pursued with his three sons for 15 years.

WHEN WAS THE FIRST HEAD-ON TRAIN WRECK IN THE ADIRONDACKS?

On May 9, 1903, the Mohawk and Malone train number 650, loaded with passengers, rounded a curve just as train number 651 was coming the other way on the same track. Both engineers jumped out of the trains before they collided. The wreck left three people dead and 28 injured.

WHEN WERE ADIRONDACK GUIDES FIRST ORGANIZED?

The Adirondack Guides Association was formed in 1891, followed seven years later by the Brown's Tract Guides Association. Both organizations helped establish uniform wages for guides and encouraged minimum standards of performance.

WHEN WERE WINTER SPORTS FIRST BROUGHT TO LAKE PLACID?

Melvil Dewey, the inventor of a system for classifying books, established a summer recreation complex in Lake Placid in 1893. He named the resort Lake Placid Club and closed its membership to Jews, blacks and invalids. In 1905, Dewey decided to add winter sports and keep the Club open year-round. He ordered 40 pairs of hickory skis from Norway and bought a quantity of snowshoes, skates and toboggans. The first guests to test the winter sports season at Lake Placid were a party of four men, five women and a child.

WHEN WAS THE FIRST HOTEL OPENED IN ELIZABETHTOWN?

Azel Abel, who had come from Massachusetts and fought in the American Revolution, bought land on the banks of the "Little Boquet" river in 1798 and put up a crude hotel made of logs. A settlement of Indians lived in wigwams across the stream, and Abel's young son Oliver often played with the Indian boys, racing up and down a trail that began near the hotel.

WHERE

WHERE WAS THE FIRST PERMANENT SETTLEMENT OF ENGLISH-SPEAKING PEOPLE ON LAKE CHAMPLAIN?

In 1761, Philip Skene, a Scotchman who had served in the French and Indian War, established a colony at the site where Whitehall exists today. He brought in 30 families from downstate New York, imported 12 slaves from the West Indies, built himself a manor house 130 feet long, and named the settlement Skenesborough.

WHERE WAS THE FIRST ADIRONDACK TRAINING CENTER FOR PRIZEFIGHTERS?

Bill Osborne, son of the proprieter of the Osborne Inn in Speculator, met Gene Tunney when they were fellow Marines during World War I. Tunney later became a professional prizefighter, and he was the first fighter to train in the boxing ring that the Osbornes built in 1926 next to their hotel. The champion trained in Speculator throughout his career, as thousands came to watch. The ring was also used by Knute Hansen, Jim Slattery, Maxie Rosenbloom, and the two Maxes -- Schmeling and Baer.

WHERE WAS THE FIRST OUTDOOR SANITARIUM IN THE COUNTRY?

The first sanitarium in the United States to treat tuberculosis patients with a fresh air cure was built in Saranac Lake in 1884. A one-room cottage painted red, it was constructed for Dr. Edward L. Trudeau, who settled in the village after he was cured of tuberculosis. During his years in the Adirondacks, the doctor founded the first tuberculosis laboratory in the world and expanded his sanitarium, where tuberculosis patients spent all their time outdoors, both summer and winter. Charging as little as $5 a week, it became a model for many others throughout the world.

WHERE WAS THE TERM FORTY-SIXER FIRST USED?

Ernest R. Ryder, a clergyman, and his friend, Edward Hudowalski, both of Troy, New York, began climbing the Adirondacks together in the 1930's. In September 1936, the two reached the summit of Dix, their forty-sixth high peak. Five months later, the Troy Record announced the founding of a new organization -- the Forty-Sixers of Troy.

WHERE WAS THE COUNTRY'S FIRST FOREST RANGER SCHOOL SET UP?

In 1912, Dr. Hugh Baker, dean of the Syracuse University College of Forestry, established the New York State Ranger School near Cranberry Lake in Wanakena. Students helped build their own dormitory, and in 1920, when enrollment was unusually high, some had to live in tents. Temperatures that winter dropped to 35 degrees below zero, and students often had to tunnel through snow to reach their classrooms.

WHERE WAS THE FIRST ADIRONDACK FIRE TOWER?

New York State began its forest fire detection program in the Adirondacks in 1909 by building an observation tower on the top of Mt. Morris in Franklin County. By the end of the following year, 20 mountain-top towers were operating. Made of rough logs and planks, these early fire towers were equipped with telephone lines that allowed observers to immediately notify rangers when smoke was sighted.

WHERE WAS THE FIRST SIGNIFICANT LUMBERING OPERATION IN THE ADIRONDACKS?

The first lumbering operation of any consequence extended along the Saranac Valley from the Saranac lakes to Plattsburgh, and in 1787 a small mill was built by Jacob Ferris at the mouth of the Saranac River. It was later sold to the Platt family, for whom Plattsburgh was named.

WHERE WAS THE FIRST PHILOSOPHERS' CAMP?

William J. Stillman, an artist and journalist, gathered together several friends and formed the Adirondack Club, which had its first summer outing in August 1858 when members camped on the shore of Follensby Pond. The group included Ralph Waldo Emerson, James Russell Lowell, Louis Agassiz, and other Cambridge intellectuals. The "Philosophers' Camp," as it was dubbed by the guides, was such a success that the next year Stillman bought a tract near Ampersand Lake, paying $600 for 22,500 acres. There he built a camp where the group gathered for two more summers until abandoning their wilderness outings after the outbreak of the Civil War.

WHERE WAS THE FIRST "TROTTY VECK" MESSAGE PUBLISHED?

Two young men, Charles Swazey Barnet and Seymour Eaton, were both stricken with tuberculosis and came to Saranac Lake to recover in the early 1900's. In 1915, while still in Saranac Lake, the two published their first volume of Trotty Veck Messages -- little booklets of encouraging maxims named after a Dickens character -- and titled it "Good Cheer." In all, 55 volumes appeared over the next 50 years. Eaton, who had left Syracuse University to enter a sanitarium in Saranac Lake, died in 1917, but Barnet kept the booklets coming. The last, "Cheery Ideas," was published in 1964, when he was 78 years old.

WHERE WAS THE HOME OF THE FIRST CELEBRITY HERMIT?

Noah John Rondeau, born in 1883, lived alone in a tiny wooden hut on Cold River in the heart of the High Peaks, where he wrote poems and kept copious journals. His life of fame began on February 15, 1947, when he was airlifted to the Sportsmen's Show in New York City. Dressed in his furs, he sold pictures of himself that he stored in his pack basket.

WHERE WAS THE FIRST SAP EVAPORATOR IN THE ADIRONDACKS BUILT?

Harvey White, a builder by trade, built a sap evaporator in Keene Valley that was used to boil down the sap from maple trees into syrup. He rented out the evaporator to farmers, who often supplemented their income by producing syrup from trees on their land. When White died, the evaporator was passed on to Allen Beede.

WHERE WAS THE FIRST CAMPSITE IN THE STATE?

New York State's first public campsite was established in 1923 on the fork of the east and west branches of the Sacandaga River, three miles below the town of Wells.

WHERE DID THE FIRST FEMALE FOREST RANGER STUDY?

In 1972, Hildegarde Kuhn enrolled as the first woman student in the New York State Ranger School at Wanakena. After graduation, Kuhn became the state's first female forest ranger.

WHERE WAS THE FIRST MURDER OF AN ADIRONDACK MILLIONAIRE?

On September 19, 1903, Orrando P. Dexter of St. Regis Falls was shot from ambush as he was driving to the post office to pick up his mail. Dexter, a millionaire who had placed fences and guards around his 7,000-acre estate, was very unpopular with his neighbors, and although everyone in town seemed to know who pulled the trigger, his murderer was never apprehended.

WHERE WAS THE PORTABLE OPERATING TABLE INVENTED?

Dr. Lyman Guy Barton began the practice of medicine in June 1839 after graduating from the Dartmouth medical college. Barton is credited with creating the first portable operating table, an invention that he developed in his Willsboro office. Until this time, emergency surgery was often performed on kitchen tables.

WHERE WAS THE FIRST ADIRONDACK FRESH WATER PEARL DISCOVERED?

In 1890, M.C. Rowe was surprised to find a pearl growing in a clam dredged from the waters of Frost Brook, a tributary of the Grasse River. This discovery was the beginning of an industry that lasted until the 1920's and produced a pearl that was sold for $1,400 at Tiffany's in New York City.

WHERE ARE THE FIRST BOBSLED AND LUGE RUNS?

Despite strong opposition from conservation groups, a bobsled run was constructed at Mt. Van Hoevenberg, six miles south of the village of Lake Placid, for the 1932 Olympics. Originally a 1.5-mile track, the run is now a 1400-meter track with 16 curves bearing such names as Shady, Little S and Zig-Zag. Since 1979, luge competitions have been held on a refrigerated, 15-curve, 1,000-meter run built especially for the 1980 Olympic Winter Games. Both the bobsled and luge runs are the first in the United States.

WHERE IS THE FIRST SYNAGOGUE IN FRANKLIN COUNTY?

The earliest Jewish settlers in the Adirondacks came as peddlers, carrying 60-pound packs of needles, pins, fabrics and small household goods. Those who settled in Tupper Lake constructed a house of worship, Beth Joseph Synagogue, in 1905. The wooden structure with its two stained glass rose windows became known as the "peddlers synagogue." In 1988, Beth Joseph was named to the national and New York State registers of historic buildings.

WHERE WERE LOGS FIRST SENT DOWN A SWIFTLY MOVING STREAM?

Until 1813, only wide rivers and lakes were used to transport logs. In that year, the Fox family sent logs down the Schroon River branch of the Upper Hudson. This successful attempt to transport timber down a fast-running stream opened vast areas of remote Adirondack land to loggers.

WHERE IS THE FIRST VISITOR INTERPRETIVE CENTER?

The idea of Adirondack Park interpretive centers, first broached by the Temporary Study Commission on the Future of the Adirondacks in 1970, came to fruition on May 26, 1989, when the first center opened in Paul Smiths. It has 5.5 miles of scenic trails as well as exhibits on Adirondack natural history.

175

WHERE WAS THE FIRST CABLE RAILROAD IN THE ADIRONDACKS?

A 1.4-mile-long cable railroad stretching up the rocky side of Prospect Mountain near Lake George was opened to the public on June 15, 1895. During its first week of operation more than 5,000 people took a ride on the railroad, which rose 40 vertical feet for every 100 feet in length. Its two cars, with seats for 54 passengers, made round trips every 30 minutes from June to October for a fare of 50 cents. By 1902 tourists were beginning to lose interest in the ride, and a year later the railroad was closed down and eventually dismantled.

WHERE WAS THE FIRST JAIL IN HAMILTON COUNTY?

In 1847, the first Hamilton County jail was built on the south side of Lake Pleasant. It offered its inhabitants home-cooked meals, a warm room and a soft bed. Inmates sometimes were allowed to work outside during the day, and once a group was used as a posse to capture lawbreakers hiding in the woods. Sheriff Frank "Pants" Lawrence, who held office in the early 1900's, once remarked that if the prisoners didn't get back to the jail by the time the doors were locked for the night "they could damn well stay outside."

WHERE IN THE ADIRONDACKS WAS THE FIRST MAJOR DEPOSIT OF IRON ORE DISCOVERED?

In 1826, Lewis Elijah, the trapper son of the Abenaki Indian, Sabael Benedict, led David Henderson, an engineer, from North Elba through Indian Pass to extensive iron ore beds at the head of the Hudson River near Newcomb. In return, Elijah was given $1.50 and a packet of tobacco. Henderson's future father-in-law, Archibald McIntyre, purchased several thousand acres surrounding the iron deposits and established an ironworks, which was finally abandoned in 1857.

WHERE WAS THE FIRST ADIRONDACK GLASS FACTORY?

In 1830, the Redford Crown Glass Works was started in the village of Redford on the Saranac River. The site was chosen because of the plentiful forests where wood could be gathered to fire the furnaces, and because of its proximity to supplies of Potsdam sandstone, used in the manufacture of glass. Master glass blowers came to Redford from England, Scotland and New England to produce window glass. From leftover melt, they created decorative objects such as paperweights, bowls, pitchers, vases and candlesticks, many decorated with lily pads.

WHERE IN THE ADIRONDACKS WAS THE FIRST ELECTRIC MOTOR BUILT?

In 1837, the first patent for a direct current electric motor was granted to Thomas Davenport, an unschooled blacksmith from Brandon, Vermont. The motor was developed in Ironville at the Penfield Taft ironworks.

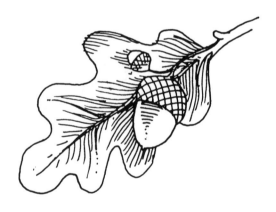

WHERE WAS THE FIRST ADIRONDACK FISHING CLUB?

In 1841, George Washington Bethune, a minister who loved to fish, formed the Lake Piseco Trout Club. Bethune, the editor of the first American edition of Walton's "The Compleat Angler," was joined by lawyers, doctors and clergymen. Wearing uniforms of Scottish tartan, the club's members were responsible for hauling three tons of trout out of the lake during the nine years that the club existed.

WHERE WAS THE FIRST FREE LOVE COMMUNITY IN THE ADIRONDACKS?

Encouraged by local landowner Orin Simpson, a small group of men and women advocating free love settled on Valcour Island in the spring of 1875.   Calling themselves the "Dawn Valcour Community," they began to practice and propogate their beliefs.   But within a few months the community disbanded, much to the relief of its more conservative neighbors.

WHERE WERE FELT SLIPPERS MANUFACTURED FOR THE FIRST TIME IN THE COUNTRY?

In 1874, a 25-year-old German immigrant named Alfred Dolge came to an Adirondack town then known as Brocketts Bridge and, in an abandoned tannery, opened a factory that made piano felts and sounding boards. More than 2,000 Germans immigrated to the town, which was renamed Dolgeville. In 1882, a shoemaker who worked in the factory began making slippers from scraps of felt. The slippers, marketed by Daniel and William R. Green, were the first in the country to be commercially produced.

WHERE IN THE ADIRONDACKS WAS THE FIRST AFRICAN-AMERICAN SETTLEMENT?

In 1846, Gerrit Smith, a wealthy abolitionist, offered black settlers, particularly fugitive slaves, the use of 120,000 acres of land near Lake Placid. Two years later Smith deeded part of his holdings to John Brown, a passionate anti-slavery advocate. Brown wanted to help support the struggling settlement, which had become known as "Timbuctu." A second, less well-known community was formed in 1848 on 200 acres near Loon Lake by Willis Augustus Hodges. This African-American from Brooklyn was the founder of the first black newspaper in the country, The Ram's Horn. Hodges's settlement of nine families, called "Blacksville," lasted only for a year or two.

WHERE WAS THE FIRST PRISON BUILT IN THE ADIRONDACKS?

In 1845, New York State officials, who had been looking for a site where iron ore could be mined by convicts, began constructing a prison in the village of Dannemora. Fifty inmates in chains were transported from Sing Sing to work on the buildings, and 40 more soon arrived from Auburn Prison. The occupants of the new corrections facility mined ore from the state-owned Skinner Mine, and in 1853 an ironworks was built at the prison where convicts were put to work manufacturing nails.

185

WHERE WAS THE STATE'S FIRST COUNTRY MEDICAL SCHOOL?

In 1812, the medical department of Fairfield Academy in northern Herkimer County received its charter as a college -- the "College of Physicians and Surgeons for the Western District." Only two other medical schools existed in the state at that time, both in New York City. During its 29 years of existence, the school graduated 611 students with medical degrees.

WHERE WAS MORIAH'S FIRST BLAST FURNACE BUILT?

In 1822 in Port Henry, Major James Dalliba and John D. Dickerson built the first blast furnace to be erected in Moriah. The furnace was a small one and turned out only 15 to 20 tons of steel weekly.

WHERE WAS LAKE PLACID'S FIRST SKI JUMP?

In 1921, the Lake Placid Club built a 25-meter ski jump at Intervale, a hill south of the village where the towering Olympic jumps were later erected. The first organized ski competition was held here in February 1921 as 3,000 spectators cheered the contestants. The next day, on a new four-mile course, the Club hosted the first ever cross-county ski race in Lake Placid.

WHERE WAS THE FIRST INDIAN TAKEOVER OF STATE LAND?

On May 13, 1974, a group of Native Americans took over a 612-acre tract of land at Moss Lake, near Old Forge. The Indians claimed that the property, a former girls' camp bought by New York State a year earlier, was once a part of ancient Mohawk territory and had been illegally usurped by the state in 1797. The new settlers tried to establish a traditional Indian community, which they called Ganienkah, but their presence created strong resentment and some violent reactions among many residents of the Old Forge region. More than three years later, the Indians were resettled on several thousand acres of land just outside the Blue Line in Clinton County.

WHERE WAS HAMILTON COUNTY'S FIRST TANNERY?

In 1820, Platt Whitman bought a tannery that his brother Isaiah had built near the mouth of Mill Creek at Wells, a site chosen because of the availability of hemlock bark, a basic ingredient of the tanning process. The industry grew rapidly throughout the area, but by the mid-1890's hemlock trees were becoming scarce, and by the turn of the century the tanning industry had left the Adirondacks.

WHERE WAS THE HOME OF THE FIRST RESIDENT NOVELIST IN THE ADIRONDACKS?

The novelist Ned Buntline, who produced more than 150 penny dreadfuls during his 50-year career, first visited the Adirondacks in 1856, when he spent the winter in an old hunter's cabin on the Indian River. After the cabin was destroyed by fire, Buntline, whose real name was Edward Z.C. Judson, traveled north and settled in a spot near Blue Mountain Lake that he named Eagle's Nest. The rowdy writer stayed in the region until 1862, when he enlisted to fight in the Civil War. Five years later, Buntline sold his Adirondack land and headed West.

WHERE WAS THE FIRST ADIRONDACK CHAIR MADE?

Looking for a comfortable outdoor seat for his family's camp on Lake Champlain, Thomas Lee of Westport built a chair in 1903 that was constructed with a single wide board for the seat and another for the back. His friend, Harry Bunnell, a Westport carpenter, produced similar chairs until 1930. The current Adirondack chair, made of wooden slats instead of single boards, is believed to have evolved from that design.

WHERE WAS THE FIRST "CHINESE JAIL" IN THE ADIRONDACKS?

So many illegal aliens were attempting to gain entry into New York State from Canada that a special jail was built to house them until they could be deported. Since most of these people were Chinese, the detention facility came to be called the Chinese jail. It was built on Elizabeth Street in Port Henry and was later converted into a tenement.

WHERE WAS THE FIRST CALICO MILL IN THE ADIRONDACKS?

In 1897, the first calico printing mill was erected in Johnsburg, near North Creek.

WHERE DID THE FIRST RAILWAY CROSS THE BLUE LINE?

Built in 1871, the first railroad to enter the Adirondacks was a short line from Saratoga to North Creek that ran along the upper Hudson River. In 1887, the Chateaugay Line was built from Plattsburgh to Saranac Lake crossing the Blue Line from the north.

WHERE WAS THE FIRST REFERENCE TO ICE SHANTIES ON LAKE CHAMPLAIN?

On February 11, 1875, in the Essex County Republican, a Westport correspondent wrote: "The bay is alive with fishers every day, and some enterprising ones have built a small house on the ice, where they can fish with a roof over them to keep the wind off, and a stove near by to warm them."